Love & best wishes Jean & John,
Christmas 1986.

from Vera & Tom

XX

MOTHER KNOWS BEST

A Timeless Collection of Maternal Wisdom

Michele Slung

CENTURY

LONDON MELBOURNE AUCKLAND JOHANNESBURG

Copyright © Michele Slung 1986

First published in 1986 by Century Hutchinson Ltd,
Brookmount House, 62–65 Chandos Place, Covent Garden,
London WC2N 4NW

Century Hutchinson Publishing Group (Australia) Pty Ltd,
16–22 Church Street, Hawthorn, Melbourne, Victoria 3122

Century Hutchinson Group (NZ) Ltd,
32–34 View Road, PO Box 40–086, Glenfield, Auckland 10

Century Hutchinson Group (SA) Pty Ltd,
PO Box 337, Bergvlei 2012, South Africa

British Library Cataloguing in Publication Data

Mother knows best : a timeless collection of
maternal wisdom.
1. English wit and humor
I. Slung Michele
827'.914'08   PN6175

ISBN 0 7126 9531 1

Photoset by Deltatype, Ellesmere Port
Printed and bound in Great Britain by
R. J. Acford, Chichester, Sussex

For
My Mother

Dorothy Helen Miller Slung

AUTHOR'S NOTE

Nothing seems to lodge in the mind so securely as the well-turned maternal phrase. Listen to your conversations and notice how frequently you offer up a maxim or a piece of advice that begins, 'As my mother used to say . . .' Most children grow up and realize, at some rather wrenching moment, that Mum is fallible, maybe not even the cleverest woman in the world, but by then it's too late—what she's said is what you've got.

Mum's sayings get repeated from generation to generation, and sometimes the original meaning is lost, yet the sense remains. Many of them are all-purpose, a few cruel, the majority loving; what's amazing is how, year in, year out, they guide our behaviour, in ways both large and small. They have no real geographic or class lines; they transcend most human divisions. All you need to do is think of one of your mother's favourite sayings, and her voice is magically in your ear.

Whether you like it or not.

KEY TO
ILLUSTRATIONS

MOTHER KNOWS BEST

I'm only doing this for your own good.

It's only your mother who's going to tell you the truth.

You always hurt the one you love.

As long as I'm around, I'll be your mother.

When my eyes close, yours will open.

You'll miss me when I'm gone.

Every cloud has a silver lining.

A little of what you fancy does you good.

You can't be in a dozen places at once.

You can't put one foot in two shoes at the same time.

Laugh and the world laughs with you. Weep and you weep alone.

You pays your money and you takes your choice.

Whatever will be will be.

If the French were so intelligent, they'd speak English.

What the eye doesn't see, the heart doesn't grieve over.

When in doubt, write a thank-you note.

A bored person is a boring person.

A doctor's never the richest man in town, but he's always well-respected.

You have to get up early to fool me.

Never trouble trouble till trouble troubles you.

Wait and see.

Jennie Jerome Churchill

Good riddance to bad rubbish.

Boys will be boys.

If you don't ask, you don't get.

Curiosity killed the cat.
Satisfaction brought it back.

When I was your age . . .

Reverse your dreams.

It's rude to point.

I'll tell you when you're older.

Klara Schicklgruber

'JUST YOU WAIT . . .'

Be careful what you wish for; you might get it.

Whistling girls and crowing hens always come to some bad end.

If I had talked to my mother the way you talk to me . . .

I suppose you think you're not going to be a parent one day too.

'I MEAN BUSINESS'

As long as you live under my roof, you'll do as I say.

I'm not asking you—I'm telling you.

That's not a request—it's an order.

Don't ask me *why*. The answer is *no*.

This is not a hotel.

Charlotte Stearns Eliot

Don't treat me like a child—I'm your mother.

If you can't stand the heat, stay out of the kitchen.

Ask me no questions and I'll tell you no lies.

Don't do as I do, do as I say.

'GO AHEAD — BE BAD'

You must think rules are made to be broken.

If you're quiet, you must be up to no good.

Your chickens will come home to roost.

You have an answer for everything, don't you?

If you tell lies, you'll get spots on your tongue.

Frances Shand Kydd

Be sure your sins will find you out.

There's none so blind as those that won't see.

A leopard doesn't change its spots.

There's no smoke without fire.

Don't Care was made to care,
Don't Care was hung,
Don't Care was put in the pot
And boiled till he was done.

It'll end in tears.

Two wrongs don't make a right.

PUTTING YOU IN YOUR PLACE

Just because parents are allowed to do something doesn't mean you're allowed to do it.

Everybody else may be doing it, but you're not going to.

Oh, so it's the egg teaching the chicken!

Don't try and teach your grandmother to suck eggs.

If you can't say anything nice, don't say anything at all.

When did your trumpeter die?

You're too big for your boots!

You're not the only pebble on the beach.

The sun doesn't rise and set around you.

You won't be happy until you're crying.

So it's raining? You're not sugar—you won't melt.

You can dish it out, but you can't take it.

What can't be cured must be endured.

Children should be seen and not heard.

There's a time and a place for everything.

When your head swells up, your brain stops working.

Mind your P's and Q's.

It's no good crying for the moon.

The bigger you get, the more stupid you are.

Nobody likes a funny kid.

If only you were more like your brother.

Fools' names, like fools' faces, are always seen in public places.

Ethel Milne Gumm

The Lady Elizabeth Bowes-Lyon

Don't be so scared—if it doesn't have teeth, it won't bite you.

Little animals don't eat big ones.

Are you a man or a mouse?

Who got out of bed the wrong side this morning?

Now you've made your bed—you can lie on it.

You're enough to try the patience of a saint.

Why do you think I have grey hairs?

You're too young to understand.

THE WORLD IS A DANGEROUS PLACE

Remember the three B's: be careful, be good, and be home early.

I wouldn't trust him further than I could throw him.

Never be in bed during a thunderstorm.

Sit in the middle of the living room during a thunderstorm.

Never walk under a ladder.

Never drink out of a drinking fountain—you don't know who's been there before you.

Always put toilet paper on the seat.

Never sit on the seat.

Put that down! You don't know where it's been!

A dog always knows when you're afraid of it.

Don't accept lifts from strangers.

Don't take sweets from strangers.

Don't go into dark alleys.

. . . And don't go near any cliffs.

Frances Zuchowski Liberace

'YOU'LL REGRET IT'

Don't cross your eyes or they'll freeze that way.

If you swallow the stone, a cherry tree will come out of your ears.

You'll be sorry afterwards.

Never nap after a meal or you'll get fat.

Don't put anything wet on the bed.

Dinah O'Dowd

Don't lean back in the seat of a train or you'll get ringworm.

You're making a rod for your own back.

If you go to bed with wet hair, you'll be grey before you're thirty.

Never learn how to iron a man's shirt or you'll end up having to do it.

Don't sit too close to the television; it'll ruin your eyes.

Never try on anyone else's glasses or you'll go blind.

Laugh before breakfast, cry before bedtime.

Cry on your birthday, cry every day of the year.

Break a mirror and you'll have seven years' bad luck.

Don't go in the water just after a meal or you'll drown.

Don't hit your mother or your hand will come out of your grave.

Sara Warmbrodt Taylor

SOME DON'TS

Don't do anything I wouldn't do.

Don't start anything you don't intend to finish.

Don't let your heart rule your head.

Don't say no without thinking twice.

Don't spoil the ship for a ha'poth of tar.

Don't expect too much and you'll never be disappointed.

Don't expect from people what they're not capable of giving.

Don't bother to get angry with people who don't matter to you.

Don't let the grass grow under your feet.

Don't sleep with the bedspread on the bed.

Don't put beans up your nose.

Don't put off till tomorrow what you can do today.

RUNNING AWAY

Is that a threat or a promise?

If you leave, don't come back.

If you leave, it's easy to show me your back,
but when you come back you have to show
me your face.

Good, I'll pack your lunch.

Lady Maud Montgomery

A TOUCH OF SARCASM

Excuse me for living.

Don't say 'she'! Who's 'she'? The *cat's* mother?

You're so sharp you'll cut yourself.

I can't shoot you—there's a law against it.

You'll be late for your own funeral.

If you get separated from me in the crowd
. . . write.

If your ship doesn't come in, maybe your
canoe will.

Has the cat got your tongue?

I'm as old as my tongue and a little older
than my teeth.

Save your breath to cool your porridge.

If she owned Iceland she wouldn't give you
a slide.

I've got a bone in my leg.

Legs were made for walking.

'YOU CAN DO IT!'

If a thing's worth doing, it's worth doing well.

Everybody has to do the best with what they've got.

Everyone makes their own contribution.

There's no such word as 'can't'.

Hard work never hurt anyone.

Grace Hall Hemingway

God helps those who help themselves.

Practice makes perfect.

You're not in competition with anyone but yourself.

You're a fool if you don't try to live up to your dreams and abilities.

There's always room at the top.

You can't keep a good man down.

Strike while the iron is hot.

Every time you give up pleasure for duty, you're a stronger person.

Don't dawdle—quick's the word and sharp's the action.

If at first you don't succeed, try, try, try again.

Abigail May Alcott

LADIES AND GENTLEMEN

A lady always has a clean handkerchief, gloves, and a hat.

A lady always has a handkerchief and pocket money.

A lady never smokes in the street.

A lady never eats in the street.

A lady doesn't swear aloud.

A skirt should be tight enough to show you're a woman, but loose enough to show you're a lady.

A lady never sits with her legs parted.

Horses sweat, gentlemen perspire, ladies glow.

Every house has to have at least one lady.

Call her a woman . . . we don't know if she's a lady.

A gentleman doesn't strike a lady.

Joanne Moore

WHAT YOU WEAR

Always put on clean underwear in the morning, in case you're in an accident.

Go ahead and try it on—you can't compare yourself to a hanger.

Who's paying for all these clothes, anyway?

I didn't buy all these clothes just to decorate your wardrobe.

Always buy one good dress instead of three cheap ones.

Margaret Majer Kelly

The important thing is to get a good bra.

Are you sure it's big enough?

An extra half-inch at the end of your hem is like an extra half-inch at the end of your nose.

Your shoes should always be darker than your hemline.

Always wear your strings of pearls in odd numbers.

Diamonds are a girl's best friend.

White is not a winter colour.

Red hat—no drawers.

Blue and green should never be seen
Without another colour in between.

Brown is a neutral colour.

Ne'er cast a clout till May is out.

Save your lace for your nighties.

It's not what you wear; it's who you are.

Fine feathers make fine birds.

THE WAY
YOU LOOK

If you want to be beautiful, you have to be willing to suffer a little.

You've got a face only a mother could love.

You'll never be an oil painting.

Pretty doesn't hurt.

Pride feels no pain.

Rachel Kempson

If you carry yourself like a beauty, people will think of you as one.

First thing when you wake up in the morning, go to the mirror and smile.

Smile and give your face a chance.

Get your hair out of your eyes.

Put some colour in your cheeks.

You're one of Pharaoh's lean kine.

Tan fat looks better than pale fat.

Don't worry—it's only puppy fat.

Sit up straight.

Throw your shoulders back and you won't feel so cold.

Clean your glasses—you can't be optimistic with a misty optic.

Wash behind your ears or you'll have potatoes growing there.

It's no disgrace to get nits, but it is to keep them.

The only thing that counts in a job interview is clean fingernails.

Wash your elbows whenever you have the opportunity.

Put on hand lotion every time you think of it.

Anna Hall Roosevelt

For every white hair you pluck out, two more will grow in its place.

Girls who pierce their ears are no better than they should be.

Nice girls don't wear ankle bracelets.

Only sluts wear half-slips.

Margaret Isabella Balfour Stevenson

AROUND THE
HOUSE

A little help is worth a deal of pity.

A stitch in time saves nine.

Close the door behind you—were you born
in a barn?

See a pin and pick it up,
All the day you'll have good luck.
See a pin and let it lie,
Good luck will pass you by.

Never answer the phone on the first ring.

Lydia Beardsall Lawrence

I don't see any hooks on that floor.

Don't put it down, put it away.

A drop of oil or a drop of spit works
wonders.

Leave a dead fly and others gather.

Sleep tight and don't let the bedbugs bite.

How can you sleep in an unmade bed?

Up the wooden hill to Bedfordshire.

Do you think your bedroom cleans itself?

IN THE KITCHEN

How come you always offer to do the washing-up at other people's houses?

Here's how you help: first you take the dishes off the table.

It's just as easy to wash a plate well as it is to wash it badly.

Always clean up in the kitchen as you go along.

It's a sin even to put breadcrumbs on the fire.

Waste not, want not.

If there's enough, put a crust on it; if there isn't, make it into soup.

The better the butter, the better the batter.

You've got to eat a peck of dirt before you die.

Take the pot to the kettle, not the kettle to the pot.

Many hands make light work.

Too many cooks spoil the broth.

Beatrice Ethel Roberts

TABLE MANNERS

Think of all the children who have no food to eat.

If you don't clean your plate, you won't get any pudding.

Bread and butter before cake.

Take the first that comes.

Leave a bit for Mr Manners.

Amalie Nathanson Freud

If you eat your carrots, you'll be able to see in the dark.

Eat your fish—it's brain food.

All the vitamins are in the skin.

The crust is the best part of the loaf.

Crusts will make your hair curl.

Eat your greens—they're good for you.

Spinach will make you big and strong.

Don't eat chocolate ice cream—it's made of leftover vanilla.

I scream, you scream, we all scream for ice cream.

Your eyes were too big for your stomach.

Don't put your elbows on the table; it'll sharpen them.

You can only put your elbows on the table when you're an aunt.

If you eat any more of those, you'll turn into one.

Don't start the day on an empty stomach.

You can't read and digest at the same time.

Thirty-seven chews to a bite.

Jana Navratilova

That's the last best bit.

Don't turn up your nose!

Only speak at table when you're spoken to.

Drink tea only out of a china teacup.

Cold food gives you a tummyache.

Serve from the right and take from the left.

Don't reach—ask and I'll pass it to you.

Don't lick your knife.

It all winds up in the same place anyway.

You're not getting up from the table until you've finished.

'LET ME FEEL YOUR FOREHEAD'

If it didn't taste nasty, it wouldn't be medicine.

Don't go out of the house with your hair wet or you'll get a cold.

Plimsolls ruin your feet.

The more you scratch it, the more it's going to itch.

It'll never get well if you pick it.

Don't stifle a sneeze.

If any germ survives that, it's your friend.

The night air will make you sick.

If you have a head, you have headaches.

Feed a cold and starve a fever.

If you don't wear something on your head,
you'll catch cold.

You're full of small ailments that other
people die of.

The best sleep is the sleep you get before
midnight.

You'll live to tell the tale.

Susan Barrantes

LOVE . . .

It's just as easy to fall in love with a rich man
as a poor one.

Throw yourself at a man's head and you'll
land at his feet.

You don't have to marry every man you go
out with.

Men are like buses—another one will be
along in a minute.

If all the girls were in the sea,
What good swimmers the boys would be.

Anyone who'd run away with you would drop you at the first lamppost.

If you can't be good, be careful.

If he tries to kiss you, call me.

You'll never get a boyfriend if you don't learn to play bridge.

Absence makes the heart grow fonder.

Out of sight is out of mind.

A bird in the hand is worth two in the bush.

When you're on a date, order one drink and sip it slowly.

A man without a good appetite for food, won't have a good appetite for anything else.

A goodnight kiss is goodbye Miss.

Save yourself for your husband.

If you had a wristwatch and used it as a garter,
When the boys asked the time you'd know just what they're after.

What does his father do?

I knew he wasn't right for you, anyway.

Cold hands—warm heart.

Don't worry, there are plenty more fish in the sea.

Pauline Koch Einstein

. . . AND MARRIAGE

Don't marry for money—marry where money is.

She who marries for money, earns it.

Marry in May, you'll rue the day.

Change your name but not the letter,
A change for the worse and not the better.

Don't marry anyone until you've seen them drunk.

Polly Scobell Cartland

There's many a slip twist cup and lip.

Men were deceivers ever.

It takes two to make a quarrel.

Like mother, like daughter; like father, like
son.

The way to a man's heart is through his
stomach.

I'm not losing a daughter, I'm gaining a son.

Marry in haste and repent at leisure.

A daughter's a daughter for all of her life,
But a son is a son till he gets him a wife.

RELATIVELY SPEAKING

Blood's thicker than water.

No matter what happens, you've always got your family.

You can choose your friends, but you can't choose your relatives.

I don't care whether you like them or not—you're related.

Eva Jagger

Treat your friends like family and your family like friends.

If you can't get along with your brothers and sisters, how can you expect to get along with the rest of the world?

A FEW
SUPERSTITIONS

Wish on your eyelash and blow it away.

Always eat the tip of a piece of pie last and
make a wish on it.

Never start a trip on a Friday.

Friday night's dream on Saturday told will
come true.

It's bad luck to kill a spider.

Anna Mathilda McNeill Whistler

Never pass anyone on the stairs.

If you spill salt, throw some over your left shoulder.

Don't walk on the cracks in the pavement.

If you drop a glove, don't thank the person who picks it up.

Don't ever talk about the future and forget to say 'God willing'.

Counting cherry-stones (who shall I marry, and when?): tinker, tailor, soldier, sailor, rich man, poor man, beggarman, thief. Or: this year, next year, sometime, never.

PROVERBIAL WISDOM

Make hay while the sun shines.

You can't make an omelette without breaking eggs.

Water seeks its own level.

A miss is as good as a mile.

Imitation is the sincerest form of flattery.

It's no use shutting the stable door after the horse has gone.

Half a loaf is better than no bread.

A fool and his money are soon parted.

You can't judge a book by its cover.

In the dark all cats are grey.

A new broom sweeps clean.

It's no good crying over spilt milk.

The early bird catches the worm.

Vera Brittain

Forewarned is forearmed.

Birds of a feather flock together.

Handsome is as handsome does.

You can't make a silk purse out of a sow's
ear.

Pride goes before a fall.

If wishes were horses, beggars would ride.

Still waters run deep.

It's an ill wind that blows nobody any good.

Countess of Rosse

Little pitchers have big ears.

Silence is golden.

Time and tide wait for no man.

ACKNOWLEDGEMENTS

I'd like to thank all the friends and friends of friends who helped: Patrick Ahern, Deborah Amos, Marian Babson, Jane Barlow, Reid Beddow, Betty Bloch, Ron Bloch, Ellen Boyers, Amanda Burden, Maurice Braddell, Taylor Branch, Joan Brandt, Sam Brown, Art Buchwald, Elisabeth Bumiller, Jonathan Carroll, Diane Cleaver, Mary Lee Coffey, Barbara Cohen, Richard Cohen, Janet Coleman, Jan Deeb, Alice Digilio, Michael Dirda, Mary Ann Donovan, Susan Dooley, Jan Drews, Nancy Dutton, Gayle Engel, Garrett Epps, Nick Eskidge, Kitty Ferguson, Pie Friendly, Harriett Gilbert, Lynn Goldberg, Bonnie Goldstein, Judy Green, Linda Greider, Christina Hammond, Rick Hertzberg, Barbara Howson, Mary Jarrett, Martha Jewett, Kathy Jones, Betsy Kane, Leslie Kantor, Stan Kantor, Steve Kelman, Meg King, Nina King, Stephen King, Michael Kinsley, Michaela Kurz, Myla Lerner, Gail Lynch, Mark Lynch, Christy Macy, Evan Marshall, Judith Martin, Kathy Matthews, Triny McClintock, Patricia McGerr, Marilyn Mitchell, Gene-Gabriel Moore, Nancy Pepper, Susan Percy, Claudine Peyre, Terry Pristin, Dermot Purgavie, Sally Quinn, Eden Rafshoon, Jerry

Rafshoon, Eleanor Randolph, Coates Redmon, George Rider, Glenn Roberts, Paula Roberts, David Rubenstein, Wilfred Sheed, Victoria Sloan, Amanda Smith, Caron Smith, Margaret Stannek, Alison Teal, John Teal, Susan Teal, Tom Teal, Val Teal, George W. S. Trow, Judith Van Ingen, Lydia Viscardi, Nicholas von Hoffman, Elsa Walsh, Jim Weisman, Steve Weisman, Celeste Wesson, Marjorie Williams, Doug Winter, Millicent Woods, Bob Woodward, Emily Yoffe.

Special thanks, too, go to: Gene Barnes, Sallie Bingham, Victoria Haines, Michael Patrick Hearn, Margo Howard, Mona Joseph, Jim Lardner, Robert Phelps, Mildred Schwartz, Louis Sheaffer, Wendell Wilkie II.